THE VOICE

For my Mother

THE VOICE

Josephine ~~Dickinson~~

To Gillian

Best Wishes

Josephine Dickinson

FLAMBARD

Acknowledgements

Some of these poems have appeared in the following publications:
*Ambit, Leviathan Quarterly, Poetry Review, Reactions 3,
The Rialto, Staple, Tideline.*

Grateful thanks are due to the Authors' Foundation for an award
made during the time of preparation of this book.

First published in the UK in 2004 by Flambard Press
Stable Cottage, East Fourstones, Hexham NE47 5DX

Typeset by BookType
Cover design by Gainford Design Associates
Cover photographs by Justine Lester
Printed in the UK by Cromwell Press, Trowbridge, Wiltshire

A CIP catalogue record for this book
is available from the British Library.

ISBN 1 873226 64 0

Flambard Press wishes to thank Arts Council England
for its financial support.

website: www.flambardpress.co.uk

Contents

Vox nihil aliud quam ictus aer

(A voice is only struck air)

Seneca, *Nat.Quaest.*, Book 2, 29

Good Friday 2001

Tonight the air
is thick with gluey smoke
as if from hundreds of burnt candles
snuffed out at one go,
and a bird rattles like a chain
in the tree.

Today they have been shooting them in the open,
lambs and ewes together,
lambs running to their mothers
as they were shot,

and Nativity has had two lambs,
cleans the second
while the first sits watching:
black chaplet, woolly crown,
red string dangling from Nativity's end.

The cool air smells of candles,
of rain, of scorched wool.
Everything is still, quite still,
except for the rattling bird.

The night is dark,
the smoke is closing in.
It smells like a small space.
It feels like a small church.
The bird rattles again.

Now from the sixth hour there was darkness over all the land.

How quickly markings vanish without trace:
the orange smudges on the wall of the race;
the pool of blood on the concrete by the gate;
the gash in the ground's side,
fluffs of wool fluttering free;
the ashes the ewes carried smeared on their heads
one morning stood at the gate;
long low mounds of smoking embers
pecked by rocking crows;
clouds and smoke trails in the sky;
snowprints;
disinfectant prints on the tarmac;
hoofprints in the mud
of sheep walking up from the wood
down to the wood and back;
the drag marks, scooped pine needles,
Visitation's final track;
the stones' switched colour with the seasons;
a creature's flit through the trees;
the lamb's grave gathering a thatch
of twigs and leaves.

But where is the lamb for a burnt offering?

The shepherd cuts knouts from their ears.
Blood spatters, drips.
They roll in corners
on shitty concrete,
twitch their tails,
wrestle with pain.
I pierce their ears
with plastic pins.
They jerk, contort.
The shepherd daubs their backs
with clotted crimson paint.

I hump one over the gate,
print its back on my front.
Red paint.
Red blood.

And when I see the blood I will pass over you.

What does the blood mean which appears
when a fat ewe lamb,
caught in the gate,
is dead when released?

But the poor man had nothing,
save one little ewe lamb.

It is the hottest day.
The lambs lie down in the shimmering heat.
But not the lamb who died.
Her head was cracked like a nut.

The wolf also shall dwell with the lamb.

The goats come in
for their evening feed,
they touch side to side
like falling leaves.

He is brought as a lamb to the slaughter,
and as a sheep before her shearer is dumb,
so he openeth not his mouth.

We drag the dead ewe through the trees,
scooping a track.
We put her on Billy's Field.
I cover her eye with dock.

Behold the Lamb of God,
which taketh away the sin of the world.

The sheep stand in rows of three,
and watch as the shepherd lures one,
until the one makes a dash
in the right direction.

A lamb without blemish
and without spot.

Families of rabbits
come out of the grass.

Worthy is the Lamb that was slain
to receive power, and riches, and wisdom,
and strength and honour,
and glory and blessing.

Ants come out of the path,
dragging grains of sand.

Hide us from the face of him
that sitteth on the throne,
and from the wrath of the Lamb.

The raised grave swells in the heat.

They have washed their robes
and made them white
in the blood of the Lamb.

The ewe's eye has been uncovered.
Something has eaten the dock leaves,
or moved them.

They have made it desolate.
The whole land is made desolate,
because no man layeth it to heart.

In the heat, we filled the grave,
found a large flat stone
to place on top,
heaving, rolling, slamming shut.

The Lions' Den

'If ever I get into the lions' den again I shall know how to get out.' D.D.

We got in the ewes and lambs
from the Flat Field without
incident, then coaxed in the Horse Pasture lot,
no, the Horse Pasture ones were first,
we put them in the race,
though D. later mixed them
all together. Big Tiny Lamb
was standing head down,
not the clamouring pet
we'd known when we'd fed
him with milk and coaxed his dam
to suckle him. She'd stamped
her feet, head butted him,
trampled him, tiny as he was,
with his one clouded eye
from when we'd found him lying
motionless on a frozen morning,
almost left him for dead, till I'd seen
a flicker of movement
and shouted to D. 'He's alive!'

Well, we got them in, then went for the tups
and hoggs on Billy's Field. D. insisted
on doing it his way, got in the pen
and poured the food while I looked on horrified
as the tups trotted in, closed the pen
gate, squashing D. who had to straddle
the trestle it was made of, very slowly,
then try to prise the gate open to let the hoggs in.

For a moment it looked as though I would have to go
and rescue him, though he'd instructed
me firmly to stay away over the wall
the other side. But he later confessed
if he did it again, he would have me there.
Then a lot of running around
with cans of citric acid and pads
of straw. At 12 the man phoned.
Then he arrived. Just a blond
in a car. Smoothing maps,
laughing the mildest words,
and not needing to see our stock at all.

A Treasure

It is a lamb's horn off a breed of sheep
no longer living here. So soft and light
when found it could have been a bleached
stem off a thistle or dock blown deep
into the wood at the height of summer.

You could sink it in a bucket of water for a day
and pin it to the shaft of an ash with a nail.
It would make a sort of shepherd's crook, but what you
        would do
with it next is more difficult to say –
tickle some creature's tummy perhaps that lay asleep.

It could be a pointing finger, or a gasping fish
whose mouth never shuts, as if the pink
interior contained too much for its hidden
spiral to hold and it all spews out
in a black rush as its streaks and lips contort.

It is peeling away from the point in strips.
It is an outer covering, has nothing to give.
It is hollow, the half bone, half horn inner core stuff gone,
and most of the pink blush worn off the ribs,
and the crown where it tore from the skull paper thin and
        white.

Another Treasure

This is a biscuit maybe, a ginger thin,
a cinnamon curl. (It is trees on a steep
hillside far away.) Its shape means something.
(There are patches of mossy green,
and on the reverse a watercolour wash,
a blur of pink.) There is something
there. (The trees climb up, up, clutch the soil
with their roots. They tremble with the effort.)
There is a right and a wrong way up.
(There are fibrous weavings, brush strokes, clearings
between the trees.) It is a mirror,
a tree dish, a thumb plate, thumb palette.
It can be smuggled in a pocket,
is the right way up.
It casts a shadow under the upcurled
lip of its curve. (Then I found another skull,
another jawbone with seven teeth,
another lamb's horn,
and the pelvis and femur of a ewe
and a set of ribs set in the ground,
a beached and buried ship.)
It is the shape of a large potato crisp.
(It is an electron micrograph
of chromosomes lined up, floating
separate, ready to go.)
It is an opaque lens. Its edges
cast shadows. Over the edges
more edges appear and more edges.
It was found in the wood in the time
of the foot and mouth epidemic.
It is probably in some sense illegal.
(It is empty fields with tufts of rush.
It is an aerial photograph
of a flock of sheep scampering to death.)

The Long Tree Fetish

The long tree fetish is a sinuous curve,
it plays one phrase over and over,
it plays it hell for leather.
Grooved paint drips,
budding studs.
It plays something simple.
It plays it again and again.
It plays it so often, it wraps a fibrous stem.
I love this tune. I'll just hum and hum it again.

All the Messages Ever Sent in the History of the Universe

Somehow, we sit on top –
frozen awhile –
till we melt, slowly drip
down the hill's side.

You sit beside the Thames,
we rills slide by.
We, though we seem the same,
change constantly.

But all the Creatures know
from that we roar,
make a great gash across
plains, what we are.

We slip to river mouths –
those, longer than
Shakespeare's tributary,
yet are nothing.

You sit and look awhile
raised on your plinth,
offer a sigh, a smile,
a let's enjoy.

These Treasures, frozen now,
all end the same.
It is the sea writes us
down in the rain.

October

Six fresh ewes stood in the shed, bewildered.
We opened the gate. They trundled through,
ran crazily here and there on the Flat Field.
The dog brought the others up from Billy's Field to join them.

Let's move, go, hie, gang, roll,
                drift, chug, explore.
I'm faint. You're a hinny. I'm not.
                Mm...Buttery. Test the sap for edibility.
This faintness...I'm groggy, hipshot.
                Hallo! Flesheater or herbivore?

Grind the cud. Dung: avoid.
                Hey! a saltlick.
Must git some belly timber,
                gobbets in ma moof.
Dabbled in the marsh. Mere pap.
                A saltlick!
Grab the grass. Sip, sip.

Time to git a nib, a quid, sugar
                her with the lump of coal on her nose.
Flat Pap dips her mush in the water.
                There's asphalt there.

Freaks!
                Jag, tug, wrench.
With nippers, winkle out,
                mumble, champ and peck.
It'll do. Just tucker.

This ewe lamb
              is in the clouds,
giddy with thinking
              of wool in the spring.
A wobbler, a blink, a dimp.

A flock of sheep like a flotilla of clouds
in the sky silently tend their grass crop in an autumn
haze. They tear at it, squeeze it, suck down
the sugary juice (not much right now), tamp
it down with pronged hooves, then fertilize
it with shit. Then wander on to the next bit.

Your Way

1

How long does it take to reach the end of the lane,
almost stationary, frozen? You tell me 'Go
ahead and feed the ewes'. I get my jar and catch
you up, take longer than I thought. But you are there
still, moving barely perceptibly, just slightly
swaying side to side. By the time you reach the shed
the sheep are fed. You had said 'Walk on. I shall be
very slow. I shall take a long time'. As distant
galaxies cross our horizon their image will
be frozen. And when you tell me to 'bugger off,
go do the job', under your rough gob is concern.
You often say 'Go on' but often I say 'No'.
For I like to walk with you, your way, more slowly
than the elephant, as a galaxy at the
end of time, faster than the speed of light, so you
are swinging out of ken faster than glances can
any more pass between, faster than I can see
any longer, than I can ever catch you up.

2

How long does it take to reach the end of the lane?
You are near the end as we watch the galaxies
fade, their appearance frozen in time. I tell you
'Go ahead, I'll see that the fire's ok', as they
recede from us. But you are there still, are frozen,
moving barely perceptibly under the trees,
your dark form gathered in the shade. As we watch the
galaxies fade, just slightly swaying side to side,
by the time you reach the shed the sheep are fed, their
appearance frozen in time. If I can ever
catch you up to taste your lips, put my arms round you,
distant galaxies will then be moving too fast.

You say 'Go on' as distant galaxies
cross our horizon. Will I ever catch up with
you? The end of the universe, frozen in time
as we watch, will never be able to reach us.

3

You tell me 'Go ahead, for they will never grow
older or change. They will only grow dimmer as
they recede from us'. Then when I come up to the
lane I expect to find it bare, but you are there,
your dark form gathered, too fast for me to see. As
distant galaxies cross our horizon, the light
they emit after the moment of horizon
crossing will never be able to reach us. As
we watch the galaxies fade, which you so often
forget, you say 'Walk on. I shall be very slow.
I shall take a long time'. You often say 'You go
on', but often I say 'No'. For I like to walk
slowly, your way, this majestic way you exist
and travel through this space on the lane by the trees.

4

How long does it take to reach the end of the lane?
As we watch the galaxies on the way back the
gob of blood glistens on the tarmac where you coughed
and although animals later lick up the blood
the dark patch stays next morning when the tarmac is
frozen. And when you tell me to 'bugger off, go
do the job', under your rough gob is concern. I
love the way you move so slowly that your mind sees
things differently. You often say 'You go on',
but often I say 'No'. I like to walk slowly
with you, your way, more slowly than the elephant,
as a galaxy at the frozen end of time.

The Lucky Penny

He watches us from the back of the truck,
his bulk shifting as the truck tilts
on the bends, as he moves from the front
window to the wire grille at the back.

Sometimes he looks ahead, at us, or
over our shoulders at the rolling,
winding hill roads. Sometimes he faces back
through the grille, picking up the ewe smells,

nostrils flaring, anticipating
November. Now he sleeps in the dark.
He stood in the ring, his bloody horn
button glowing neon. The blood streams,

stanched, converged on that spot on his head.
It was his second time in the ring.
The first, his one near whole but blunted
horn still curled, and he was bid for and sold.

Then he left the ring and, it is said,
with a crack fragmented horn from head.
The sale was cancelled and he returned.
This time he made a hundred and ten,

less six – the vendor's lucky penny.
Like a rather portly gentleman
standing at his window, admiring
the view, he knows that he has many.

Where Were You When I Came in
from the Evening Milking?

Where were you when I came in from the evening milking?
Your chair sat empty by the fire, its cushion hollow,
And each room in the house was empty also.
Where were you?

You were not in any of the house's rooms.
I looked carefully in each one.
And the window view each looked out upon was empty.
Where were you?

The mossy garden path stepped empty round
the corners of the house.
Thyme, ramsons, rosemary leapt in the breeze.
Where were you?

I thought I glimpsed you once in your cap, slowly shuffling on,
face down, intent on the cobbles.
You did not see me – the light shone through and you were gone.
Where were you?

I stood outside the house and looked in where the sun shone
from the west straight into the mirror.
I thought for a second you were standing there.
It was not you, it was the setting sun.

The Memory of All the Times I Ever
Spoke to You

Sometimes in town, at the end of a long lane lined with cars,
there's a sudden patch of green.
Next to the stile where the footpath starts
– almost hidden – you can just make out
the ragged grass through the gate,
the dandelion heads' fluff.

Where are these places in the town? You would find them all.
They are few and far between.
Concrete covers the greater part,
though narrow strips of grass still sprout
in the cracks and where allowed:
a building's bit of rough.

You'll catch just a glimpse and then it's gone, like a doomed
    ship's flare.
If you turn and pass again,
the chances are it'll still be there.
Or then, again, it just might not –
or the sun's gone behind a cloud,
or you don't know where you are.

Sometimes you'll stop the car, if you can, to have a stare,
to hold, a minute, the green
flash, with eyes scrunched against the glare,
blurred with sweat if the weather's hot,
or if, despite the sun, it's cold,
fumbling back a tear.

And sometimes, if there's time, you walk along the path
to the gate and peer inside
at the fuzziness there of seeds and bees,
at the matted stalks crackling underneath,
and you set a foot in the grass,
then another, and you're in.

And then you are alone. You breathe the softer breath
one needs to breathe to hide
in a wilderness of grass and trees
that remembers life in the fief of death.
Did it take me and my voice?
Is this the place I'm in?

Where are those hidden places? Will you ever find them again?
When you're in some dead end lane
will you turn and catch a cranesbill blue
or a devil's bit or a marsh mallow
in the corner of your eye?
Or did the wilderness die?

To Music

You think that I've deserted you,
for human hedge and rabbit run.
You owl, that I've deserted you,
your wooden words and well swept house.
Well, I have left your house, your art,
chopped down the bridge, veiled out the view.
But know I'll stem the river's tide,
you'll grow your legs, ignite your eyes,
and so, I hope, undramatise
our river bank communion.
No bridge will drop us, river drown –
our hearts are twain, our love is one.

The Touch

Do they know, with what sense
they have of touch,
– know, that is, without discs, corpuscles or nerve-ends –
that I'm going into their heart,
going where fingertips, palms, lips cannot,

into their inner whorl,
their chamber, their
heart, genitalia, toes, arms, head, hands and tongue,
their nipples and tissues in the
chamber where counter-rotating spirals

steal their treasure and make
their face into
treasure such as is accessible to pressure
of light on the skin, on the eyes,
light on a long, gradually curving trail?

Semaphore of the Tongue

semaphore of the tongue
a candle an open fire
a candle an open fire
continually
a cesspit and a well
the lost ship has sprouted colours
letting go they stood
business is bad
a cesspit and a well
chew
her hands are grubbing
for hours in green
to you?
on the platform
aluminium hoardings
a cesspit and a well
taste the powdery coal of hell
pleasure is not the word
yards and yards of blank
with a gasp every second or so
my Virgil
my Beatrice
Catullus
kissing is not the point
at chess
taste the powdery coal of hell
stood still
the maze's
for hours in green
a candle an open fire
channels wolfed us down
kissing is not the point
money's not the most

clown smile
the red and blue
important thing
she lacks nothing
may I cling
bye bye Dionysus
she contains all
in a square in Bruges a clown

If You Have Not Wanted to Lick
the Piano Concerto

If you have not wanted to lick the piano concerto
(of course I am and going) with their tongues
of fire, and to think that such is human life,
the more I see you the more I want you. Somehow this
damn thing, so gorgeous is it, then you to the movies
or explaining about nothing or to be born, to work,
to love, to become more mad about you,
more lost without, have never felt that physical impact
of paint eating an apple, concerto piano.
No 'should' and no blame. The continuity,
grow and to disappear as if desirous to lick
the kettle, you, and so it goes. Can you imagine.

Annunciation

The sky clears.
The sun melts the ice.
You are cruel.
But I hold you close.

The sun changes.
Your eyes are blue.
You are cruel.
But your words are true.

I am wishing blessings down
upon three ewes to go for mutton,
one of them Susan
or Annunciation.

I ask you can you hear her voice?
You say she's wanting out on the grass.
Well of course!
That would be the cause.

You stand at table writing THREE
GELD CHEVIOT EWES FOR SALE
D.D. (I ponder writing J. AND D.,
but thereby hangs another tale.)

Farewell to Samantha

Up the Horse Pasture I walked,
through the buttercups and cuckoospit.
I found her grazing alone.
I stroked her downy belly,
ran my fingers over her hard
flat nose, her velvety mouth,
scraped a nail through the cross
in the straggle of her back,
looked into her fathomless
wet peat eyes.
I sat under her chin
and let her chew my hair.
I ran my fingers up and down
her forelegs till clumps of down
drifted away. She paused,
then continued to pull
and surround with her mouth
the tufts of grass. I turned
and walked back. She followed,
keeping to her own worn furrow.
I turned her out at the gate
and enclosed her in the pen,
then gave her a bowl of barley and maize,
and a bucket of water.

The Golf Ball

For some reason she was lying near the door
when she awoke. It was still dark. She woke up
in the hay, but not in the bed she'd built high
up near the rafters, but low down by the door.
In the lamp glow the first thing she saw when she
awoke curled up on the warm sweet hay was three
little alabaster suns glowing in the
hollowed out hay. (She looked up to where, high up
in the roof, on the bank of hay, a makeshift
bed of roughly levelled bales was half hidden
from view by two bales stacked end to end.) She reached
out her hand to touch and they were cold. She tried
to find her shoes. They weren't visible, but in
the lamplight she saw the three eggs. Then she saw
it. The golf ball, white and dull in the same nest.
A monster of sterility. Outside, there
was the softest glow in the Eastern sky, like
the shine on burnished silver. Barefoot, she picked
her way over the sharp cold stones of the yard.

Sheila and Jack

I jumped up naked, then remembered –
Douglas had said 'Wait here.'

The couple stand in the window
looking at Scarberry Hill. I run
back to the bedroom, don some clothes
before they can see me. They've been expected
this past six months, and now they come
this afternoon and find us in bed!
They knock at the door. It's answered
by their cousin in bath towel, using
the first excuse that comes to his head,
i.e. we're in the bath, just a mo,
we'll get some clothes on, do come in.
Meanwhile, I'd assumed all clear, but no.
I straighten shirt, go in, kiss both.
A moment of awkwardness, then sweet-
ness and light. We all forget the 'bath'.
(It barely, if at all, improves the truth.)
Crisp polka dots is like her cousin's mum
I think. Her better half slumps in red,
still gobsmacked. I put on all my charm.
Chat re. her cousin as a lad,
the girls when small, hols at the farm.
Swimming at Barnard Castle (not bad,
twice a week for eighty-one or so).
The brothers lost in the war. 'Sad times'
she says. Then raspberries: they grow
them by the bucket. Would have brought more
had they only known their cousin
is no longer alone. They gulp and stare
as the full implications of
the afternoon's events sink in –
as they assess me for the walk on part I'll have.

The Bargain

If saying I am deaf can make it so,
and we must not admit you're eighty seven,
and you think not I might not hear you go
today when, cold and tired, you leave the garden
suddenly (I'm staking wire against
the rabbits with Raymond, you say 'Three's a crowd'
and slip away, enticed by pipe and stove,
I stay and splice the jagged netting ends
with bleeding fingertips, alone), and love
does not convince us, either, we have good
intentions: deafness then can be my one
defence, your age becomes a toothless weapon.
For, deaf, I hear, approve, forgive your laugh,
and you in turn have cut your age in half.

The Voice

The door clicks open.
I hear a voice.
A window shudders.
Waves crash.

The voice I heard
last thing the night
my hearing died.
A hum and a hiss.

A goodnight kiss.
In the garden tonight
I hear your voice
as you open the gate.

Out of the air
a voice without a face.
Not ocean currents,
and not Antarctic ice.

The voice incites to prayer
in the wilderness.
You whisper
the prayer.

Ossicles hammer the sounds –
malleus, incus, stapes.
You whisper
'Goodnight.'

A Murder

Her father and her best friend
(every hillside was painted
with autumnal colours)
in a children's playground
discovered her body
(rocks and bracken)
on The Common
on September the Fourteenth.
(Then I came upon
a group of chanterelles
that were beautifully
fresh, yellow and edible.)
Police released a man aged forty five
and a woman of forty two
also being questioned
(not an easy thing to locate in mid-September)
in the hunt for the killer.
(After that there were more
treasures, but all the time
I felt a little unhappy
to be down there
in the gloom of the trees.)
The girl, fifteen, was found
stabbed and mutilated, two
hundred yards from her home
(down there in the gloom
of the trees, while I could see
unending sunshine gleaming
on the slopes above).
That evening she had gone out to post
a letter, but never came home
(and took to the hills).
Her friend discovered her body
lying beneath a slide.

(It was the well known
Fly Agaric, the big poisonous toadstool
that has a scarlet cap with white spots.)
She never came home.
DNA samples were taken
from up to eight hundred men
(a rare moment of autumn warmth and sun).
Stabbed and mutilated two hundred yards from home
beneath a slide
(unending sunshine)
her home beneath a slide.
She had gone out that evening to post a letter
but never came home.
Painted with autumnal colours, my way
led up through steep woods, past a
succession of splendid waterfalls.
A youth, nineteen, of The Common,
will appear before magistrates in the morning.
No sooner was I out among the rocks and bracken
but I was rewarded by the high spot of the day.
I watched potential predators and potential prey
sharing a rare moment of autumn warmth,
a rising column of warm air
(not an easy thing to locate in mid-September).
Gradually they spiralled ever higher.
She never came home.
There were cheerful voices overhead. I looked
up to see twenty five choughs circling and playing in the sun.
DNA samples were taken
from up to eight hundred men.
Mushrooms and toadstools were on my mind
when I set off on Monday morning.
There were many fungi under the trees.
A man of forty five and a woman of forty two
are on bail pending further enquiries
into offences of assisting an offender,
officers said.

The first I found being the most spectacular.
It was the well known Fly Agaric.
She had gone out that evening to post a letter.
But never came home.
I followed the track gently upwards
for a long time, but eventually
it curved up into a high shadowy valley
I had no desire to enter.
Keeping in the sunlight, I traced
my steps down to the woods
and the thunder of the waterfalls.

That Was the First Time I Ever Saw Your Face

The tracks cross each other in the snow. What does it mean to meet you, him, someone, anyone? The creature at the end of the track. For a long time wheels zigzagged, two passed from the right, swept in a curve. I did not see your face till the weight swung towards the middle foreground, and one. You were upside down. Hidden by the moon and the stars. No. That was me. To centre, found line crosses back from the left to the right. The tracks cross each other. Road much further. None appear to keep straight ahead – they two pass from the right, sweep round, right arm on right knee, then thought are further from the creature in rays to the left than the creature is to the sun. Feet on ground. Angels' wings down. And one from left to there then clear. The eyes hid like creature afraid. Right sense. A whole bundle of nerves. Winking lights follow the predator overhung, others kept straight, bunched up, under sharp sky. Clouded with iron, sharpened. Half on the right, half on the left. All dark, find smell, light, to a point draped with softness. But I'm still upside down. Knock. How cold sweat seeped. They were still further.

Many feet came to a stop. All the feet stopped. Then a moving muscle twisted to know. Then a grain of sand to the sun at the zero hour that was walking that way. Creature. Soul's distance from you. That for which their tracks turned. Walk through dark. The tracks melt in the sun, as they melted, were on the screen, turned to lasers, tunnelled to a shrewd pinbright grey. The rough peaks become smooth. The rough bits smoothed. Eyes mopped, surface shiny then translucent. Light went through. Lights down. And the lights went down under hair. This was no longer a surface. Omega point. A few knobs turned, long silence. Settle in – the colours cleared. It was first of all white and rough, what I saw. The scale of popcorn. Very pleasant, short, then blank, then became rocks and mud. Was no longer white. Words and breaths in between. Blank. And what's this? A colour? Catching at excess of oxygen. Accommodated to the availability of light. Blazing logs as the plate of horizon, rocks and mud of self, warm smoke. Which, while we stood, fell and span. You escaped, yes, for a few moments. Accommodated eggs in a basket. Ha. Settling into a rattle, to the availability of light, struggling to maintain its spin. Each of its two tips raised like a wing, a plate of land in the distance, settling after a fall. Still vibrating, trying to spin. Each of its two horizon tips raised like a wing.

41

Stupid and Crikey

Her black hair glistens.
Sweat stains silk.
Wolves in the rain
Are hunting the elk.

She sees you, listens
To your camera voice.
I can't. It's dark –
Though the wide screen glows.

My earholes roar.
My mouth is cracked.
You stiffen the arm
I try to touch.

This hartshorn for her –
I took it for me.
It has left me in a stupor.
Wake me.

Why Didn't I Think of Saying That?

'what is the word – ' (Samuel Beckett)

The suits at this meeting would
have stopped to listen. Their pens
would have clattered into silence.
Their mouths would have dropped open
as if to catch a choice morsel of food.
Sheets of paper would lie ignored.
Then they would stretch their lips
in a smile and there would be a flutter
of quickly clapping hands.

It would have wiped the smile off the face
of that man in the blue tie who has
studiously ignored me all morning.
Every time I speak he parts his lips,
holds his right hand in a drum-ready
position and waits, eyes dipped, as if
about to say 'Have you quite finished?'

Instead, they taste the air with their chins.
They shake their heads and chew their pens.

The Face

The flat tones, the urgent tones hard by his shoulder,
stooped on a low chair in the infant school
under the pinned up kiddies' paintings,
tight-lipped, his chief card at his right,
does he remember what he felt when he heard that voice,
as he saw his future before him, the future,
the past being somewhere else, lost in a classroom
in the history books that totter on the shelves,
and he in a blue shirt, a cranberry silk tie,
a black suit, a close crop of lightly peppered hair,
the world knows, the world remembers the face –
does he remember the voice?

the voice of the aide at his shoulder that we can't hear,
whose frozen echo is still out there somewhere?

Colors Are Different Now

Colors are different now, the rainbow straight and blue
and green. Twenty blocks north the thousands died, two
weeks ago, in wind which swung to south, including three
hundred and forty three firefighters, two guides, twenty
officers and four sections. Then burnt plastic cabling,
climbing harnesses, helmets, knee and elbow pads,
crates of torches, helmets and safety goggles, clothes,
batteries and boots, cartons of cigarettes, gum
and candy, tables of soft drink and food, unopened
boxes of TVs and CD players arrived.
Coffee, cigarettes and ice were all they wanted.
'This way for massage. Prayers and spiritual guidance:
third floor.' Tar, metal, burnt plastic, cavities, heat
and fumes. One hundred and one thousand tons are shifted,
one hundred million tons of rubble still to go.
The towers were one thousand three hundred and sixty
feet high. And the smoke stopped and the flow of people
stopped, the running people stopped, the blue sky started,
the past tense started. One hundred and ten storeys.
'1.58pm GMT jet crashes into tower.
2.16 jet crashes into second tower.
2.43 jet crashes into Pentagon.
3.07 second hit tower collapses.
3.25 car bomb explodes in Washington.
3.27 first hit tower collapses.
3.30 another jet crashes near Pittsburgh.'
'It is dark like snow.' They speak of how many 'worked'
in the World Trade Centre. 'Thousands of people or
an unknown number worked in the World Trade Centre.'
'Let terror twist the world!' He was in a restaurant
nearby, and a plane flew low. There was something wrong.
It was flying too low. A lot of pigeons flew up.
'Is there anything I can do?' 'There is nothing
anybody can do. There is nothing any
body can do.' 'I love you too. I'll come home safe –

45

don't worry.' 'We work too hard, we're not paid enough,
and we're all ill' – foreman at Sultan's mine (Sultan,
fourteen, thinks he's lucky to have this job). Father
Judge's morning prayer had been for 'Peace and joy
in our city'. Hollow eyed, blinking, they emerge,
after a night cowering, nowhere to run. The sky
streams, the window streams. Unseen enemy, nowhere
to hide. We are tired. Heavy. No sleep. Sick at heart.
Streaks across the sky. 'Fallen blossoms had drifted
into the corners like snow.' I will sleep under
the sky rather than stay in the city. 'There were
peaches, plums, apricots, pears, apples, quinces, cherries,
walnuts, mulberries, pomegranates and vines, all
growing in one garden. There were also nightingales,
blackbirds, thrushes, doves, to raise their notes, and chattering
magpies.' Huddled in buses and trucks at a bus
station just after dawn children shiver in the
cold early morning breeze. A man is holding his wife
in his arms. He sits cross-legged on the ground. She sits
between his knees. His arms engulf her. Looking closer,
I see her face appear four times more. Once in the
crook of his right arm, once in the left. Once beside
herself. And once, without hat or hair, in the depths
of his groin. 'It is the Americans, the A-
mericans!' – a little boy crouching in an air raid
shelter in Afghanistan. Three thousand five hundred
refugees arrive over the border at one
station alone. What is their state? Pathetic – that
is the only word for it. They have fled for three days,
have come without food or belongings, have had nothing
to eat for three days, have come for aid, food, protection
and shelter with the poorest of the poor. Some of them
are existing on mulberries. There is nothing else.
There were many lush orchards and fruit trees in the old
flourishing Kabul. Alexander Burns visited
Kabul in the 1830s. 'The gardens are well
kept and laid out, the fruit trees planted at regular
distances. The ground is covered with fallen blossoms.'

'We had no sleep last night. We were all night running
in and out. The children were crying. In the end
I had to bring some of them to safety. Some of them
are still back there.' An eleven-year-old Northern
Alliance soldier grins, shows off his Kalashnikov.
'I've killed many Taleban with this.' A songbird
with green feathers is killed in an American
bomb attack. A seventeen-year-old Northern Alliance
soldier has escaped from the Taleban. His friend
has not. 'I ran away, but he could not' he says.
Dery Gul did speak last night. From her hospital
bed she told staff simply 'I have lost my children.'
'Moral strength will defeat terror' says Tony Blair
and the Americans step up their bombing campaign.
'What shall I do now?' asked the mother of seven
killed in Kabul on October the twenty eighth.
'Look at their savageness. They killed all my children
and my husband. The whole world is responsible.
Why are they not making a decision to stop?'
'My children, they cry all the time. It never stops'
said Zarmeen Bibi in Kabul. 'I have lost all
my family. I am finished' said someone else
as other women hugged her. 'My husband, my son,
I have lost all my family. What can I do?'
Fatima Gailani said 'Kabul was a happy
place when I grew up. Everyone lived in peace and calm.'
'They are targeting our houses. Why do they do it?'
There are kinds of flowers – puspawarna – two of nine
of which stand for a mood of ripeness and fulfilment
during the final hours of the all night puppet show,
the wayang kulit. People smile at each other while
the music wafts around. They step over the sarons
as musicians play through the night, the night which swells
to giant watermelon size. When the gong sounds
their eyes meet and they smile, they join hands
and talk till the thin line of the rebab comes round
again and then the gong sounds and it begins.

Jesus at Easter 2002

When Jesus appeared in a dream this Easter,
the Easter of the attack by Israel on Ramallah,
I'd thought he was dead. I hadn't expected to see
this stranger's golden mane and laughing eyes.
He'd just died, they said. I'd arrived too late.
But when he squeezed me in his arms
and I said how can you do this when you're dead and why
don't you do this more often, Jesus? he replied
I'm busy right now in my birth town, Bethlehem.

You thought they were all dead?
I don't care how they were.
You gotta check with more care.
If any more of that scum
make it to Beit Jala from Bethlehem
it will be the worse for you.
Open the ambulance door.
Stick 'em all. If you see any more
you know what to do.

(You'll be saying Jesus was dead next.
But, as we all know, he came back.
Lord of the Dance my arse! Alive – what a pain –
he ponced round kissing the women,
shaking his golden mane. He was laughing!
– the playboy – when they begged him
to keep coming back again.
He'll be too busy now to bother with them.
He'll have stuff to do in Bethlehem.)

The Chair Animal

after 'Das Stuhltier' by Paul Klee

At three o'clock in the afternoon
the dizziness became too much.
The clap of fan, crack of whalebone,
grizzle of daytime faded
while he applied shoe black, pretending
to be at seminary where
he was the local wire-puller,
enjoyed the look of shock on faces
when he defied the ban on, of all things...
So he picked up his fiddle, became
a musical mastaba stuck in the desert,
except he was hungry as a gled
and scared of the murk the shiny japan
couldn't hide, albeit brainless,
and the fiddle felt more like a lampadist's
torch as he concentrated on one spot
of dung in the distance, which if he had
the knack to remove... They were killing
the fatted calf for him when he came round,
but there was some taboo on talking.
He watched them strut and he could strut.
His temper cracked; they tried to push
him like a truckle. That was it:
the watchet stars exploded, he could
crank his booty like a cox.

The Dugong

The dugong chubs the tropic green
in great fat mouth dunked in the sea.
He's got the film star touch: his hunk
of trunk is specially designed
to look like nude fish tailed colleen
to brine crazed sailors; but to me
his sawn off jowl suggests the punk,
the bullet eyes fierce pride of kind.

Angelica

Under the weight of heads
the stems droop low, the creamy
efflorescence spiders
slowly prickle through.

Umbels, petioles
expand.
Lower stems
sink lower.

Forks have split and swollen.
Water jewels
stud their skin.
Rubbed, they remain.

After the storm
heads sweep the grass.
Great limbs lean close,
their hollows give.

Lower leaves
two or three times pinned,
come autumn, crackle and dry,
as brown seeds pepper the soil.

In wet and ice floods
angles become acute.
Angelica leaves. Her plundered
seed heads drown.

On the Wind

in primis venerare deos, atque annua magnae
sacra refer Cereri laetis operatus in herbis
extremae sub casum hiemis, iam vere sereno.
tum pingues agni et tum mollissima vina,
tum somni dulces densaeque in montibus umbrae.
      (Virgil, *Georgics*, I, 338–342)

(Important: respect the powers that be,
as you work on your cheerful farms.
Burn sheep for the food Boss yearly,
at winter's end, as the spring sun warms.

It's then that lambs are succulent
and the last year's wine mellows.
It's then that sleep is seductive
and the mountains crowd with shadows.)

17.2.01

A white shape passed by.
I had thought
it was dark outside.
We sat and talked.

The sounds continued
after she was gone –
ghostly voices
wafting into the evening air.

I paused,
but, seeing nothing more,
continued
exactly as before.

25.2.01

They were better before and after
than they were when it was still.

26.2.01

Over the dark world
I stand tall.
I curl into the air,
cherish all,
wrap around
every wisp of air,
spit its fragrance into the sky.
Am I death?
I give life,
alchemize.

I make music,
warm and lighten,
speak,
cleanse.
It is what you want,
after all.
I am a caged beast,
obedient.

The French have seen it,
yes: it is the virus
builds pyres,
drags carcasses
by the leg
and glows all night.

The fires are burning tonight,
not starlight,
not moonlight,
but a roiling wound of fire,

an earthspot,
earthspots,
hellholes.

Do not worry.
People
are immune.
'Mum, why
don't they say
what would happen
if humans got it –
presumably the same?'

When the spring comes
it will bring pain.
The grass will grow bright
ungrazed.
Barns will be empty.

In France a day-old lamb,
head bent back,
knifejacks
on a mountain
of wool.

The angel of death passes over the land.
Who knows if today will be their last
to tend their herd or flock,
the last day of their history,
the last day of the wind, the rain, the light
reflected through a newborn creature's eyes?

The black faces, feet, dash down the lane,
then are gone.
The emptiness has a meaning,
not a normal absence.
But they are back again
in an hour,
swirling tails
under the swooping pairs of birds.

Will we see their lambs?
Will their lambs live to see?
To open their eyes
at the moment of birth,
to stand on their feet,
eyes open,
as few of us do
in a life?

The bird in the top of the tree,
shaking it one way then the other,
says whatever the future is it is.

Farmers feel
spine tingling fear
as the stories
close in
and they huddle in
their inner rings with their shuffling
beasts.

Over the fields
the fires advance,
Hephaestos prints,
millennium beacons.

Ash Wednesday

We all go that way,
in the sun and the sky,
a wide green field like a sea,
and above it the sky,
the rears of sheep
roll towards the horizon.
Why do they run so fast,
why?
They are lighting beacons in the sky.

Roads empty, town empty.
The unity of knowledge.

A circle closes in,
a tightening loop of string.

The dog barks.
A walker rushes past
on the other side of the lane.

The sun is here,
glints cold, metallic,
hard, cuts spring out of year.

Whatever was vibrant
is gone.

Making tea I push my woollen sleeve under the grill
to fetch out a plate and recognize the smell of singed wool.

The news bulletins go quiet.
The post man comes again.

All around are
scampering feet,
darkness and fear,
while here
they are scurrying,
dust around their feet (meat).

A large farm near Penrith they say, 7,500 sheep –

get your head round that.

No, it was 9,700 sheep,
371 cattle...

7.3.01

These sheep push against my body,
their solid bulk displaces mine,
their wet wool discharges gushing
moisture into my garment.
Little bobbles of snow get stuck
between.
They are in the same space.
At the edge of two lives
they are reaching in.

'(It depends what you mean by a field doesn't it?)

Yes it is in a garden.
Yes there are sheep on all sides.
The risk is there.
But I am allowed through.'

It's best, the best thing
is just not to care
too much about anything
anymore.

For the first time the birds sang,
for the first time the snowdrops showed,
weak and sparse.
Look carefully:
they are still there.
But so is the coil
that snakes over the wall
down the path to the wood
from the yellow government truck.

And now that government policy is failing, has failed,
they talk of the prick.

Farmers ask if they could preserve
blood lines built up over generations,
ask if they could keep one animal,
but all such requests are turned down.
Every day they change their minds on people:
'Last night I rang farmers and I could hear
their wives crying in the background.
The ministry is destroying animals
that are perfectly healthy from herds
that date back to 1850
...were told they had a confirmed outbreak...
they were distraught...was sobbing. She said
she couldn't live this way with all the dead
cattle around. It was torture.'
Mr Hodge said he had been told that when carcasses were
left for days in other areas of Devon scores of rats were seen
streaming out of them.

The dog leash lies on the floor
where the children left it weeks ago.

There's a prickle in the nose,
the sting of formalin.

The two big boys stand looking at us,
wondering why we are looking at them
with anxious fondness.

11.3.01

Things are grim,
it's on all sides,
it's closing in.

There are worrying rumours that sheep on either
side of the road near Hartside summit
are suspected. D. says they are well over
on the other side of Hartside top.
Well, a couple of miles.

Then the news that Langwathby is hit.
That's Bibby's out.
So, Carr's at Hexham it is, or nothing.

12.3.01

Snow muffles the road against us.
Fields are empty, fields with woolly studs,
fields with flocks at home,
a field with a hayrack which sheep climb up
and on our return are still climbing up.
They are carrying on their private lives
as we pass through
dousing wheels, hopes,
snatching mealfeed, tools,
and heading home
with a blank cheque to despair.

The evening star is clear and far,
the sky is blue and calm and true.
Below the houses start to glow.
The flashing yellow
trundles down the Hartside pass,
and when it stops it looks like fire.

There are miles upon miles of empty fields.

'It is a bereavement, the worst
thing after losing a husband, or a daughter.'

They are sending in the army
to shoot them on the fells.

D: 'I am beginning to find it frightening.
I thought of putting the four hoggs and a tup
in a safe place. But it's not allowed.'

13.3.01

Guns are being taken from farmers
too desperate.
There is a shortage of shepherds
('well you can't pay them on what
you get for an animal')
to bring them, to nurse them,
watch them on the fells.

'In the old days they had them up there.
A horseback rider would drive
them back up the Fell every day.
It was known as the three o'clock turn.'

Sealed lorries,
terrible convoys.

They are saying it is now out of control
in Cumbria.

Long, low black clouds float
over the horizon in the western sky
under the evening star.

Left out there to lamb on their own
they die an awful death.
What can we do?
We can do nothing.
There is nothing we can do.

In the past there were the famous
seven plagues.
Now here are two plagues
from Britain.

The gnawed stumps
of thistle ends
are chewed back to the ground.

A ewe quietly grazes
on the skyline.

Slaughter on suspicion...
what does it mean?
that a farmer must pronounce
death sentence on his own.
It means witch hunts,
holdings-off.

On this beautiful blue sky morning
muddy black clouds hang over the west
and smear the east.

'There should be a lot of spring life
on this farm and there isn't going
to be any.
    It's empty
        the farm's
            the farm's.........' (farmer sobs)

14.3.01

Foot and Mouth locations
The 222 confirmed outbreaks of...

For seven days and seven nights
it burned.
God's own county.
They can't get their sheep home to lamb.

Under the evening star
the sky is scorched.
An ugly black band of cloud
bolts the horizon,
rising in a plume that tails off at the end.

They step up the slaughter –
3,500 healthy pigs in Northumberland,
2,000 in France.

'It's gone dead.
It is cold and quiet.
There's nothing happening.
It looks bleak.
I look around and see all these fields. They are empty.
They will be empty for months.'

Black gauze hangs before the clouds.
The mucky red clot in the sky
plumes over from the SW
against a sickly orange glow.
The fells beyond are crystal clear,
so it's a clearer day than usual, but
the smoke chokes it.
Bits break off it like shit.

A burnt offering.   I conclude that God
A Mass.   must like sheep very much
Offertorium.   and wants a lot
Agnus Dei.   of them in Paradise.

Columns of white smoke,
wide at the base
(not the thin winding streaks of heather fires)
rise up from the fell.
There is no wind,
but fine dry flakes of snow
in the sudden chill.

In the foreground black face ewes graze oblivious, content.

15.3.01

Ben Gill: 'There will be many tears around the British countryside today. Our farms should be starting to jump to life with newborn lambs and calves. Instead many will feel that spring has been cancelled and their farms are simply "dead".'

Dusk falls.
Another day.
How many more
plumes tonight?

Scarlet soot
veils the clouds.
Canopies of it
billow over Scarberry Hill,
where, at the top,
the last light blazes,
an angry, apricot wound.

If it isn't successful –
and God forbid that –
where does the killing stop?

'He (Mr B.) said the Government hoped to devise a strictly controlled plan to allow expectant ewes and cows to be moved so they could give birth.' They'll be sure to hold on for that.

16.3.01

7.00am
'They're going to kill a million sheep today'
(a hollow boast).

'Alston is neither fish nor flesh (sic)
(fowl?) nor good red meat.' D.D.

The sky is muddy grey,
not the sort of cloud seen on the fells.

8.00am
'The farmers are going to revolt.
 The farmers are going to demonstrate.'

The Government want to 'return the countryside to normal
life within ten days'.
Normal life? Normal?

'The cull has been ordered by ministers who are intent on
returning the countryside to normal life within ten days.'

The sheep crowd down by the fence and graze.
They carry a flask, a flagon full to bursting point.

5.30pm
Long muddy clouds float past like garbage tugs.
SW a speech bubble barb.
A bright blue sky day.
And an acrid stink barbed in the throat.

Nick Brown still does not respond to a request for an
interview after three days.

7.00pm
J: 'I feel passionately for the farmers.'
D: 'I feel passionately for the lambs that are being bumped
off as soon as they are born.'
(The hard-nosed, frostbitten farmer speaks.)

A sheep farmer's diary:

4. 'The sheep Joe's really worried about are the ones on the
open hills. These sheep are 'hefted' – taught by their mothers
where to roam so, like a good Cumbrian (says Joe), they
never stray too far from home. You couldn't replace this flock
in the event of foot and mouth, or they'd just wander off.'

64

5. 'Listen.......all you can hear are the birds.
There's just no one about in the Lake District at the moment.
The footpaths are closed...the silence is almost eery (says Joe).'

10.00pm
There's a shortage of vets, and fuel for the pyres is running low.

They finally openly say '...this epidemic'.

'Newsnight':
Nick Brown, scared and dogged, at one moment says it has
been spread through markets and by the sheep farmers, no
other way, and we have contained the spread, at another that it
is going from farm to farm, even hopping farms by wheels or
people. I expect we just don't know.

He insists he is acting on the advice of professionals, not on
personal political opinion.

He claims he would have nothing to advise the PM about the
date of the election.

17.3.01

Clouds continue to roll off the SW horizon,
muddy, flat bottomed, bubbling.

'Nick Brown has backed down.
The RSPCA have written
to say he's killing the wrong sheep
for the wrong reason.'

9.00am
A lorry struggles at the bottom of the
street where the town cross meets the high.
A Co-op lorry pulling in for a delivery
is what I assume as I sit back
ready to wait behind the wheel, decide
where to park, when to set off.

'It's one of those lorries' D. says.
I look closer.
Yes it is. How did I not recognize it?
It comes like death –
dark grey, low slung,
creeping,
cab inscribed:
'Let the chicks run free'.
The driver waves to me
soberly as the massive bulk
inches past.
How heavy it is, how crammed
inside with raw flesh destined
for the chopper and the boiler
in some distant town.

More smoke fills the valley.
Over hang great canopies,
great tents of smoke,
sombre marquees.

They even
seriously moot
culling flocks of starlings –
if it were any use.

18.3.01

'They'll be sick up in the hills.
They'll be feeding their sheep knowing that
tomorrow they will be killed.'

Gentle snow comes like millions of soothing hands,
soft crush ice.
Under the grey snow clouds
the ewes come down for their food.

In the glorious sunshine
black smoke pours down
the Blackburn valley.

And Alston is sunk in blue again,
under black chalky clouds
layered upon each other,
up and down and back.

Today I have a feeling that it's in Alston.
I don't know why, I dreamt it, and feel I know it –
somewhere, now.

Behind, in front
of Scarberry Hill
clouds hurry
from South to North,
their colours
never seen before:
cherry purple,
burnt rubber, wool.

Over the wall a flock of black face ewes
prepares for the night,
a dark assemblage, eating at the hay
rack, sitting, grazing, looking.

19.3.01

The ewes are still sitting quietly
in the morning light and frost.

Over the lane
a single ewe
comes down
to the fence
to look for one
of their number loose
from the night before.

No sign of the missing ewe, no tracks in the snow.

D: 'It's been blowing drifts in the night
and all the shepherds will be hunting their sheep.'

Empty fields in the valley
where the pregnant ewes should be
shine a gunmetal bronze through the snow.
Where are the sheep?
They are trapped in the hills.

Image of Mr Brown in an aircraft seat smiling,
reading the papers, chatting to his secretary.

They talk of shooting heavily pregnant ewes,
of the lambs alive inside as a problem...

Another brilliant sunny day with strange black clouds.

D: 'This is special. I've had a long lifetime
and it's never happened like this before.'

One side of the lane is an empty field,
where this morning ewes were grazing.

On the other side,
where ewes often sit serene
like a family on a picnic,
a ewe on her side
paddles her legs feebly in the sunshine.
'She's at the end of her tether – she's an
old ewe' D. says.

A spiral of black fluffy clouds
winds up from behind Scarberry Hill
as the dying ewe convulses
and twitches and her sisters spread out
grazing without pause for thought, for rest,
for anything.

Every night it's still the same evening star
rising still and bright behind the smoke.
If only there were a word for above, behind,
beyond.

'I got out of bed to cry.
I got out of bed because
there is nothing to go to.'

'Yes I would say we have it under control,
we have it contained in areas.
We need farmers to help us
control it.'

They say they will carry out this 'firebreak' over the next few
weeks, even that they will start it in the next few weeks.
But what if the disease does not stand still in the meantime?

20.3.01

In the pre-dawn dimness
the shape of the ewe cast
on her side is flanked by the others
lying asleep.

She is still alive. As the pigeons
start their cooing and her fellows stir
and look and begin to nibble at the hay
her legs are twitching.

As the apricot plum smoke
settles in the Blackburn valley,
the morning sun creeps across the dying ewe.

There are 100 cases in Cumbria.
Today the mood has changed.
Melmerby and Ousby are barely ten miles away.
The field next to Billy's Field is empty of its last few sheep
(tups?) today.

The field on the south side of Bleagate has a few sheep.
Eliot's field has a few sheep by his farm.
That is all.

And the cast ewe
lies quite alone,
legs barely stirring
now and then.

There are a few bronze cows down in the NW.

A tower of silence
rises up behind
Scarberry Hill,
a great pillar of smoke.

'When he came to Cumbria,
England's most beautiful county,
what he found was the distress
of farmers' (re. Wordsworth coming to Dove Cottage).

21.3.01

It is getting nearer. Melmerby
and Ousby are only ten miles away.
The burning smell at dawn
gets stronger.

The trusting ewes come to their usual
place for the night under the garden wall
where their dead or dying companion still
lies. But for how much longer?

I think she is dead. The only thing that moves is her fleece
in the wind.

The sky is sharpest blue.

Last night there was film on the News of slaughtermen in white robes stunning and killing cattle. They said they can kill a cow a minute. Our little flock of sheep would take – how long?

7.15am
D: 'The trees should be budding.'
J: 'I don't hear the birds sing.'

They know there is something wrong.
The Government have their mind on the election.
It's at Melmerby – ten miles away.

D: 'Oh, it won't be as much as that, as the crow flies.'

The valley fills up with a haze of smoke.
Details of the river bed visible miles away
show it is a clear day.

She is dead.
She has that sunk,
heavy look about her.

'It is a hard life but a great one'
(Will Cockburn).
'We mustn't give up –
people two miles from it
are not giving up.'

Lakeland farmers say if they try to cull their breeding stock they will release them and let them take their chance on the fells. The Ministry and its dogs will never be able to gather them up again.

We can but aspire
to the total prostration
of death.

The burning is constant.
'They see the funeral pyres
from miles off –

they don't see what goes on
in here.'

22.3.01

The snow falls silent and steady.
There is no wind.

At first I hardly see her.
She is blanketed in snow,
folded in.

Their heads are smeared
with ash today –
either a sign that they will die,
or that this plague will pass them by.

'Republic of Ireland, Roman Wall.
We do not know where we're
going' (Ben Gill).

Huge tracts of land will be cleared of their livestock.
They are staring in bare fields.
The ewes are about to start lambing.
We will love every lamb.

It's out of control, sweeping across.
They asked to have a minister for Cumbria.
He said he would become that
minister.

Paula: 'What a responsibility.
It's practically a sure thing
that we'll get it, isn't it, really?'

Sheep – limps of rag on a sea of mud
cannot be moved.

In mourning.   Silence.

Our ewes are marked with the ash
on their foreheads.

The farmer can do nothing except
watch his sheep die in frozen fields.

Another ewe is as dead in the field
near the garden wall, flat on her front.

23.3.01

It's a month of madness.
Hetherington just lost 5,000 sheep.
How long till it gets into the hills?

Another dead ewe.
Or the second one above
has staggered to the wall and collapsed
unseen, legs splayed behind.

'I didn't watch them put on the fire but I did
see the smoke the next day. And then tears did come to my eye.
The cattle were my friends. It is getting to me.'

More pictures appear of slaughtermen
putting the bolt on their head like chrism.

D: 'They won't want it on the Fell.'
J: 'What they want won't come into it.
    This disease does not respect people's wants.'

The car is full of choking fumes.
The wet gloves sting
from squirting the wheels.

25.3.01

Melmerby. Ousby. Milburn.
It's getting frighteningly
close.
And the sheep up on the Fell
go free.

26.3.01

Inger says it's only a matter
of time –

(but we can hope).

'There won't be a single sheep or pig or goat or cow
left in Cumbria.'

Nick Brown says they have already killed and incinerated more
animals than in the '67 outbreak. So they must be doing alright.

D.D.   'We have foot and mouth.
        Tommy rang. It's a mile or
        so away. Gilderdale. Over the
        other side of Scarberry Hill. The vets
        were there all morning.'

It is three miles as the crow flies.

On the News they showed the 2.5km pit they are digging.
That's where they may want
to put Little Lamb...

The Government doesn't know
what to do next.

7,000 sheep were buried today
and the army hopes to bury 10,000
tomorrow.

There are few boundaries here
on the fells.

What do you think?
'No wagons, no wagons,
no machinery coming.
Slaughtered and disposed of,
we would settle for a man with a wagon.'

27.3.01

There's a rumour –
Oh my God
where's it at?

99% sure
up Hartside Road
next Alan.

Wanwood Fell.
Shall we look on the map?
No – I've walked it:
Gilderdale,
Wanwood House.

Alston is like death.
In the Post Office you can
hear the stamps flipping.

The postmistress is dead or has
forgotten to wake up, frowns grey
and heavy.
It's terrible, terrible.
Her eyes say it all.

A large truck turns left
on to the Hartside feeder road,
stacked with huge round bales of straw.

In those low sprung container lorries
the sheep sleep and dream:
as they are tipped out like mucus
spat out of a blocked throat
they are leaping to freedom.

'When you go over Hartside Top
you can see sixteen fires burning.
And there are piles of
sheep carcasses – the smell is
dreadful, you have to switch
off the heating.'

A stone grey pall hangs over
Scarberry Hill.
Behind it lurks
the first outbreak.

Hope! hope! hope!
'I feel very, very sad
about giving up my flock,
but if it is going to help
my neighbours it has to be.'

'Outbreak...epidemic':
almost 400,000 animals
have been slaughtered.

A storm swoops down over Scarberry Hill.

At Great Orton
they are erecting pens and sheds
for the slaughter of animals:
'It will be a challenging day.'

Herdwicks in the twelfth century
escaped shipwrecked galleons
of the Spanish Armada. Landed Cumbria,
survived snowdrifts by eating
their own fleece.

You see fires everywhere.
You see men with guns slung
over their shoulders.
You see people living in fear.

28.3.01

Finally get through to MAFF website.
'There is a case at Wanwood
at a field near...ref. on map.'
D. says it is far away, near
Kirkoswald.
So we are alright.
There is hope.

'I couldn't find Allingham – as far
as I know there's a Methodist church
and nothing else – he maybe had
his sheep on sacred ground.'

It's an invasion.
And this enemy replicates.
'A(dd)llingham is a folly – it's a chapel,
a Methodist church – and not much else.'

The empty fields begin to green
slowly, ungrazed.

People who always have a twinkle
in their eye look dead, withdrawn.

The rushes stand silent, still.
No animals come to the edge.
No animals come down to look.
No shepherd rides a quad up the track.

Our sheep look up, and at the moment of eye
contact spread their ears over and out
like angel's wings.

The blackness
chokes the sky.

The killing of healthy sheep
has started today.

Twenty people and two vets
in a vast white tent.
The sheep, they say, are fed
and watered on arrival,
before being taken through
to the slaughter tent,
presumably because,
if they were not fed,
they would make too much noise.

They 'only disposed of
6,000 animals today'.

We need a Dr Life not a
Doctor Death.

Jackson: 'I never like to see death. It's the waste – I mean,
it's the waste. I mean, I eat meat, I'm sure most of you do,
and it's such a waste.'

They have gone mad – they are killing rare breeds in
adventure parks, gentle alpacas and merinos in wool farms,
scrambling to slaughter as many animals as possible.

And Blair is asking people to go to the countryside, the show
goes ahead, the census goes ahead, the damn elections are set
to go ahead, while everywhere people are desperately trying
to avoid spreading infection.

29.3.01

'I'm going over the Fell.
Tonight I'm going over the Fell.
Tomorrow I'm going over the Fell.
All the time I'm going over the Fell.'

He pulled the plug on the phone,
threatened with the pan,
threatens all the time,
threatens the pills.

The words are not the whole story –
the words nearly always go with violence,
or the threat of it.

A black lamb and a white lamb
are born in Rodney's Field.
The black one nimble on its
feet, gambols and sucks, the white
one sits exhausted for a bit until
nuzzled by its mother onto its knees
and then onto its feet.
She looks up at me. She
fusses round them, takes a bit of grass.

Further down the fields is an
older black and white lamb.

Above them a storm
rolls down enfolding Cross Fell and
the valley.

The use of vaccines is 'approved'.
Is MAFF up to it?

'Newsnight':
It has been found they are not
following guidelines set up
after the 1967 outbreak.

The world is running crazy.
The sheep are lying peacefully
over the garden wall.
They are talking about vaccinating
cattle in order to export them!!

D. cracks and says – 'If we lose
our sheep we're not getting any more.
I'm finished.'

They are digging more trenches in Cumbria.

Under darkening skies
there is little to lighten the spirit –
diggers claw the piles,
tractors begin to move the carcasses
from the farmyards where they died.
Pyres burn all around Okehampton.
There are patches of sunshine.
Fields are deserted, their stock
awaiting of transport to a final
destination across this fertile farmland.
More pillars of smoke.
Villages circled by destruction.
Emptiness that extends
every mile –